Animal  Lives

SPIDERS

Sally Morgan

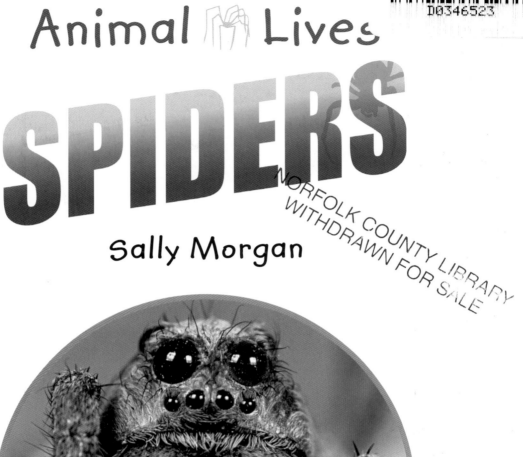

QED Publishing

Copyright © QED Publishing 2004

First published in the UK in 2004 by
QED Publishing
A Quarto Group Company
226 City Road
London, EC1V 2TT

www.qed-publishing.co.uk

A Catalogue record for this book is available
from the British Library.

ISBN 1 84538 301 X

Written by Sally Morgan
Designed by Q2A Solutions
Editor Christine Harvey
Map by PCGraphics (UK) Ltd

Creative Director Louise Morley
Editorial Manager Jean Coppendale

Printed and bound in China

Picture credits

Key: t = top, b = bottom, m = middle,
c = centre, l = left, r = right

Ardea/Nemesia Simoni 21 /Duncan Usher
28–29;
Corbis/Anthony Bannister 22, 24t, 30 /Terry
Whittaker 16 /Hal Horwitz 19, /Joe Macdonald
30t, /Pat Jerrold 10, /Malcolm Kitto 25t; David
A. Northcott 27;
Ecoscene/Alan Towse 27b, /Chinch Gryniewicz
13, 30, /Kjell Sandved 15b, 24b, /Robin Williams
13t, /Wayne Lawler 20b, /Sally Morgan 19,
/Robert Pickett 7, /17;
Getty Images/Kevin Schafer 12t, /Davies &
Starr 16 /Steve Taylor 17b, /W.B. Irwin 17t, /
Al Satterwhite 18, /Tony Bennett 18, /
Carol Farneti 14.

The words in **bold** are
explained in the Glossary
on page 31.

Contents

The spider

Many humans are scared of spiders, with their eight long legs and hairy bodies. But spiders are fascinating animals to study.

Spiders belong to a group of animals called arachnids. Arachnids have four pairs of legs, eight eyes, a pair of fangs and a body divided into two parts – the **head-thorax** and the **abdomen**. Spiders' legs have joints so that they can bend. Scorpions, mites and ticks are also arachnids.

Joint

spider

Spiders have a collection of short hairs on their feet. These allow the spider to walk upside down on ceilings and over glass.

fact

4

A spider's body is divided into two parts.

Leg

Pedipalp

Eyes

Front part (head-thorax)

Rear part (abdomen)

Claw

The spider's armour

The spider's body has a tough outer covering, a bit like a suit of armour. This is called an **exoskeleton**. It protects the spider.

Spiders are unusual as they can make silk. Many spiders use their silk to make webs.

All spiders have eight legs.

Types of spiders

There are at least 40 000 species, or types, of spiders. They vary greatly in size and appearance.

Among the smallest species are money spiders, which are less than 1cm long. The giant spiders are the tarantulas. These spiders have bodies up to 12cm long! Although they look very frightening, not all of them are poisonous.

The body and legs of a tarantula are covered in hairs.

spider

The largest spider in the world is the goliath birdeating spider. It can be as much as 30cm across when its legs are stretched out!

fact

Jumping spiders

One of the largest groups of spiders is the jumping spiders. These jump to catch their **prey** and to escape **predators**. There are also groups called wolf and huntsman spiders that do not make webs.

Other groups include orb web spiders, such as the garden spider, that weave a circular web of silk. Some orb web spiders have brightly coloured, spiky **abdomens** to put off predators.

Huntsman spiders run after their prey on their long legs.

Jumping spiders lie in wait and then leap onto their prey.

Where do you find spiders?

Spiders are mostly land-living animals and live in almost all areas of the world. The only places they do not live are the cold polar regions.

This spider has spun its web across a window to trap flies.

Spider habitats

Spiders live in a great variety of **habitats**. Most spiders are found in forests, woodlands and grasslands. These are places where there are lots of animals, especially insects, for the spiders to prey upon. They also live in caves and deserts. A number of different types of spiders live in our homes, too.

Raft spiders are found in wet habitats with small ponds and streams.

Living in water

There are a few spiders that live in and on water. For example, the water spider lives in still and slow-moving water. The raft spider lives in marshy places and can run across the water's surface!

spider

Spiders are good to eat! The Piaroha tribe in Venezuela roast goliath birdeating tarantulas over hot coals. They don't eat the fangs, but they use them as toothpicks.

fact

Finding a mate

Spiders need to mate before the female can lay her eggs. First the male has to find a female. Sometimes the female releases chemicals, like perfume, into the air to attract a male.

The smaller male spider signals to the female spider.

Attracting a female

Spiders use different methods for attracting a mate. Male wolf spiders drum on the ground to make **vibrations** and some orb web spiders drum on the web. Some males dance in front of the female: they raise their front legs and twitch their **abdomen**.

spider

Some orb web males bring the female a gift of a fly wrapped in silk. They mate with her while she is eating her meal.

fact

Danger

Mating can be a dangerous time for male spiders, because they are often killed and eaten by the female spider.

A tiny male Nephila spider approaches the much larger female.

11

Beginning life

This female spider has wrapped her eggs in a cocoon of silk thread.

Female spiders usually lay their eggs at night. Some female spiders lay a small number of large eggs, others produce thousands of eggs. All spiders lay their eggs inside a protective **cocoon** made of silk.

spider facts

• Some spiders can lay 1000 eggs in less than 10 minutes.

• Garden spiders may lay 9000 eggs, but only 200 will survive to adulthood.

Hatching

The spider **larvae** hatch from the eggs at the same time. They break out of the eggs using a special egg tooth. They stay inside the cocoon until they have grown larger and it is safe for them to leave.

Spiderlings are tiny when they hatch from the eggs.

Moving on

With some species of spiders, the **spiderlings** move onto a special nursery web made by their mother. Some female spiders catch **prey** for their young to eat. After several weeks, the spiderlings move away and live on their own.

Wolf spiders make a nursery web for their spiderlings.

Growing bigger

Spiders have tough **exoskeletons** which cannot get larger. To grow, the young spiders have to **moult** their exoskeleton.

When a spider is ready to moult, it hides in a safe place. It hangs in the air on a thread of silk, or turns over onto its back. Gradually its old exoskeleton gets loose and splits open. Then the spider pulls its legs out of its 'skin', just like we pull off gloves. Its new exoskeleton is soft at first and the spider can stretch its body to grow. Then the exoskeleton becomes hard.

Some of the large tarantulas may moult 40 times in their lives.

Reaching full size

Each time a spider moults it gets about one-fifth larger. Larger spiders have to go through more moults to reach their full size. After the last moult the spider is mature and ready to mate.

15

Making silk

Spiders can make silk using special silk glands in their **abdomen**. They make long, dry threads called draglines, which they lay out behind them as they move about. Many spiders make webs from their silk.

This orb web spider sits in the middle of a silk web.

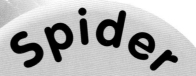

spider

Silk is unusual because it is not attacked by bacteria or fungi, so webs remain for a long time without rotting.

fact

Flying

Small spiders and **spiderlings** use their silk to fly. They release a strand of silk that is caught by a breeze and lifts them into the air. They can be carried over long distances this way.

Silk is liquid in the spider's abdomen. When the spider releases it, it becomes solid and forms a thread.

Trapping prey

A different, sticky silk is made by spiders to trap **prey**. A non-sticky silk is used to wrap up the bodies of their prey once they are caught.

This Indian ornamental spider has lined its burrow with silk.

Spinning webs

Many spiders make a web to catch their **prey**. Each type of spider has a different way of making their web, but they are usually spun at night.

A spider starts by spinning a thread that becomes attached to a branch. Then it lays another thread to form a 'Y' shape. The spider then moves to the middle and spins threads that look like the spokes of a wheel. Finally, the spider lays a sticky thread in a spiral from the middle to the outside. It is this sticky thread that catches their prey.

Orb web spiders often place their webs across open spaces between bushes to trap flying insects.

18

Catching prey

Many spiders wait in the middle of their web. Any prey flying into the web gets stuck on the sticky threads. When the prey struggles it makes **vibrations**. The spider feels these vibrations and rushes over to catch the prey before it can struggle free.

Calico or Nephila spiders spin huge webs that stretch several metres across.

Hunting spiders

Some ground-living spiders do not spin webs. They hunt their **prey** instead. Most of these spiders hunt at night. Instead of webs, wolf and huntsman spiders hunt using their long legs to move quickly across the ground.

Crab spiders wait in flowers for insects. These spiders are coloured white, pink or yellow to match the flowers.

A crab spider has caught a butterfly.

Spitting spiders hunt by releasing a jet of silk.

spider

The crab spider is named after the fact that it moves sideways and that its legs are held out to the side like a crab.

facts

Spitting spiders

Spitting spiders are unusual. They can make silk in their head as well as in their **abdomen**. They mix **poison** in with this silk. Then they sneak up on their prey and squirt two jets of sticky silk over it in a zigzag pattern so that the prey is stuck to the ground.

Poisons

Spiders have jaws, or fangs, that inject **poison** into their **prey**. Some spiders have a poison that kills their prey. Others have a poison that just **paralyses** their prey.

Hunting spiders simply catch their prey and bite it. Web spiders throw silk over their prey to trap it first before they bite it. Then the prey is crushed and wrapped up in silk like a parcel. They may store their prey and eat it later.

A spider has two fangs either side of its mouth.

Spiders hold their prey while they bite with their fangs.

Eating prey

Spiders have a small mouth and they cannot swallow large prey. They pour chemicals over their prey so that it becomes a liquid. The liquid is sucked up through the spider's mouth.

Spider senses

Spiders need to have information about their surroundings and they get this from their senses. They have a number of different senses, including sight, touch and taste.

Most of the hairs on a spider's body are connected to nerves. The hairs are very sensitive to **vibrations** and air movement, so spiders can detect the lightest touch. Hairs on their first pair of legs are sensitive to taste: often spiders decide that they don't want their **prey** after tasting it with their legs.

Trapdoor spiders hide in their tunnels and jump out at prey.

Each hair can sense changes in the spider's surroundings, such as air movements.

Raft spiders extend their legs onto the surface of the water to sense any vibrations caused by insects.

Sight

Most spiders have eight eyes, although a few have six. The hunting spiders, especially the jumping spiders, have very good sight. However, in many spiders sight is less important than their other senses.

spider

Jumping spiders are the only spiders that react to their own image in a mirror. They move into a threatening position, just as if they were facing another jumping spider.

fact

Spider movement

Spiders can run quickly thanks to a long leg that is made up of seven parts. There is a joint between each part of the spider's leg, and a spider can bend its leg at each joint. This means a spider's leg is much more flexible than our legs.

The long legs of the huntsman spider help it to run quickly after prey.

spider

fact

This spider raises its front legs by pumping fluid from its body into its legs.

Moving legs

Spiders move their legs by **contracting** muscles. They have muscles that move their legs inwards, towards their body. However, they do not have any muscles to move their legs back out again. To stretch out a leg, a spider has to pump body water into it.

Spiders under threat

Many different types of spiders are threatened by the loss of their **habitat**. In Britain, for example, heathland is disappearing. Two of Britain's rarest spiders live on heathland – the raft spider and the ladybird spider.

Another spider under threat is the red katipo spider. It lives on sand dunes along the coast of New Zealand. The sand dunes are being disturbed by people using the beaches. They are also being cleared to make way for homes. As a result, this spider is decreasing in number.

The ladybird spider has a bright-red abdomen. It's one of Britain's rarest spiders.

spider

The Kauai cave wolf spider lives in lava caves in Hawaii. It is threatened because lava is being disturbed by the building of new tourist hotels.

fact

Caring for spiders

Sadly, many people do not seem to mind if spiders become rare, especially if they are poisonous. Spiders are not as popular as some larger animals, such as lions and tigers.

This makes **conservation** of rare spiders more difficult. It is important that people are taught that spiders are just as important as larger animals.

Life cycle

Female spiders lay eggs, which they wrap up in silk to make a **cocoon**. Sometimes the female spider carries the cocoon around with her.

Some female spiders guard their eggs until they hatch.

Tiny **spiderlings** hatch out of the eggs, but they stay in their cocoon for a few weeks until they are larger.

Young spiders have to grow larger by **moulting**. Spiders have to moult many times to reach their adult size. Once they have moulted for the last time, they are ready to mate.

Spiders moult to reach adult size

Eggs covered in silk cocoon

Spiderlings hatch out of the eggs

Glossary

abdomen the rear part of a spider's body

cocoon a case made of silk spun by female spiders to protect their eggs

conservation to protect and preserve valuable wildlife habitats and all the animals and plants that are found in them

contract to get shorter

exoskeleton the tough outer covering of a spider that protects its body

habitat the place where an animal or plant lives

head-thorax the part of a spider's body to which the legs are attached

larva (plural larvae) a young insect or spider, it often looks very different from the adult

moult to shed an exoskeleton and replace it with a new, larger one

paralyse to prevent from moving

poison harmful, toxic substance

predator an animal that hunts other animals

prey animals that are killed by other animals for food

spiderling a newly hatched spider

vibration a to-and-fro movement

Index